GERMAN PHILOSOPHY

UNTIMELY MEDITATIONS

GERMAN PHILOSOPHY

A DIALOGUE
ALAIN BADIOU
JEAN-LUC NANCY

EDITED AND WITH AN AFTERWORD BY JAN VÖLKER

TRANSLATED BY RICHARD LAMBERT

THE MIT PRESS
CAMBRIDGE, MASSACHUSETTS
LONDON, ENGLAND

First published as *Deutsche Philosophie: Ein Dialog* in the series Fröhliche Wissenschaft at Matthes & Seitz Berlin: © MSB Matthes & Seitz Berlin Verlagsgesellschaft mbH, Berlin, 2017.

This book was set in PF DinText Pro by Toppan Best-set Premedia Limited. Printed and bound in the United States of America.

Library of Congress Cataloging-in-Publication Data

Names: Badiou, Alain, author. | Völker, Jan, editor.
Title: German philosophy : a dialogue / Alain Badiou and Jean-Luc Nancy ; edited by Jan Völker ; translated by Richard Lambert.
Description: Cambridge, MA : MIT Press, 2018. | Series: Untimely meditations ; 11
Identifiers: LCCN 2017060981 | ISBN 9780262535700 (pbk. : alk. paper)
Subjects: LCSH: Philosophy, German. | Philosophy, French. | Discussion. | Badiou, Alain. | Nancy, Jean-Luc.
Classification: LCC B2523 .B3313 2018 | DDC 193—dc23 LC record available at https://lccn.loc.gov/2017060981

10   9   8   7   6   5   4   3   2   1

CONTENTS

GERMAN PHILOSOPHY

The following dialogue took place on January 30, 2016, as part of a conference at the Berlin University of the Arts (UdK). Thanks are due first of all to Alain Badiou and Jean-Luc Nancy for accepting the invitation to participate in this wide-ranging debate, and for their willingness to revise the resulting transcription. They also agreed to respond to two further questions (on Adorno and the contemporaneity of philosophy), which are included in the following text. Funding for the conference was kindly provided by the German Research Foundation (DFG). Finally, special thanks are due to Alexander García Düttmann, who played a key role in making this dialogue possible.*

VÖLKER   I'd like to begin with a very general question. For both of you, German philosophy plays an important role in your works, as does the question of the timeliness of philosophy, that is, the timeliness of its intervention in the present. How would you assess the state of the philosophical relationship between France and Germany?

BADIOU   In my view, philosophy exists in a discontinuous manner. I believe there are certain philosophical periods.

*[A number of people helped to bring the present translation to fruition. First of all, I would like to thank Paola Ghetti for all her advice and support during the course of the translation. Many thanks also to Céline Cantat for generously taking the time to comment on certain passages in the text. I am also grateful to Jan Völker for his helpful and considered responses to my queries. Finally, my thanks to Marc Lowenthal and Anthony Zannino at the MIT Press for all their assistance throughout this project.—Trans.]

The idea of a continuity, a tradition, is in any case an academic idea. And as for the idea that the human being is a philosophical animal, that philosophy exists always and everywhere—that's a platitude of contemporary journalism. There are discontinuous philosophical periods, and we can locate them historically. There was, of course, the great Greek philosophical period. There was a great Arabic period, appended to this Greek period. In the seventeenth century, there was a French period that began with Descartes and included Malebranche, Spinoza, and Leibniz—even though Leibniz was German and Spinoza a Flemish Jew. At the end of the seventeenth century and the beginning of the eighteenth century, there was an English period with Locke, Hobbes, and Hume. Then there was a German period that we now know as German Idealism, with Kant, Fichte, Schelling, and Hegel. And it seems to me that in the twentieth century there was something like a Franco-German period, which revolved around phenomenology. It began quite early, with Husserl, and then Heidegger, and in France we had Sartre, who went to Berlin just before the war, and Merleau-Ponty. What we are seeing today is perhaps, and I'm taking a risk here, the end of the French period—or "the French touch," as the Americans say, who contributed much to its academic popularity. And if we look a little closer, this is perhaps also a Franco-Slovenian period—let's not forget Slavoj Žižek and his followers. As I said, this period began with phenomenology and particularly with a complicated relationship to Heidegger in Derrida, Lacoue-Labarthe, Nancy, and Ricoeur. It continued through

French structuralism, as marked by Lacan and Foucault in particular ... and sitting before you now are two late representatives—two survivors—of this approach.

So what was this French period, which began as a Franco-German period and then became increasingly French until it came to represent France in America? It was, I believe, an attempt to establish philosophy in what I would call a new place. The aim was not to circumscribe philosophy in an academic fashion, but rather to relate it to its outside in an extremely vital way, to nourish it on literature, painting, cinema, mathematics, and psychoanalysis, while also breathing new life into the vitalism of Nietzsche and Bergson, as Deleuze did. In this way, all of these thinkers sought to establish a renewed critical role for philosophy, with close ties to the political. There were, of course, different tendencies. There was Derridean deconstruction. There were the postmoderns, like Lyotard. There was the Strasbourg school, with Lacoue-Labarthe and Nancy. And then there were more individual endeavors, such as my own, which I would gladly describe as neoclassical. In sum, then, the philosophical relationship between France and Germany passed through a period of great exchange and proximity between the 1930s and the '60s, or a little longer—in any case over a long time that, rather remarkably, included the Second World War.

So where are we now? I'd say we are probably at the end of this period. And we don't know where we are going. There is great uncertainty about the fate of philosophy in general, especially where the Franco-German relationship is concerned. In fact, it seems to me that the question of the state of philosophy today, as reflected in the Franco-German relationship, is one that will depend on you—I mean, in light of where we are holding this discussion, on you young Germans, but of course also on those young French people who are interested in philosophy.

Before I finish, I'd like to add that I have long been in favor of the fusion of France and Germany. I'm not a great champion of Europe. What is Europe, ultimately, without Russia, without Turkey, clinging to a defensive and rather uncreative relation to its former imperial grandeur? No, what I'd like to see is the fusion of France and Germany. One single country, one single federal state, and two main languages—that's quite possible. France is an old country, crushed by the weight of its history, shriveled up and conceited for no reason. Germany, on the other hand, is a very uncertain country. It doesn't know what it is; it's desperately looking for itself, and always has been. If we were to fuse France and Germany we would put an end to dear old France and give Germany a real youth. And what would philosophy be then? Well, I think it would be truly Franco-German. And that would perhaps be its most glorious period of all. That's my contemporary myth.

NANCY There is first of all a paradox here. We are discussing philosophy between France and Germany or the Franco-German philosophy of Alain's prophecies, and yet we are French—how strange! But perhaps not as strange as it might seem, since I think that between the two of us there's something very subtle, barely visible, which is marked as a form of French sameness, yet also functions as a difference between "more France" on the one hand and "more Germany" on the other. I don't know if you would agree with that, but …

BADIOU   So I'm too French and you're too German?

NANCY   Too? *Warum nicht*? I don't know. In any case, I think I can follow the historical path you have sketched quite clearly, but I would add something to it and at the same time change its trajectory a little. Where you said, "despite the war," for example, I would tend to think that it wasn't despite the war but rather precisely because of it. In other words, France in fact became philosophically more German during the interwar years, with the introduction of Hegel into France by Kojève, the proximities between Bataille and Heidegger (which aren't well known, but they do exist), and many other such factors. I think it's no coincidence that with the onset of the First World War—which was the first great shockwave, the beginning of the end for Europe—a sort of intersection emerged that was essentially marked by the importation of German philosophy into France, which until then had remained curiously unknown. It wasn't that the means of communication were lacking, but there was ultimately little transmission of ideas. The Second World War then saw the departure of a number of philosophers from Germany, and at the same time, just after and even during the war, the invigoration of French thought by what was coming out of Germany.

Yet I think we can also trace these phenomena further back within the history of philosophy you outlined. We could add that it has often been said of the great German Idealism—and, incidentally, of early German Romanticism—that it marked a contrast with France, because in France there was a revolution while in Germany there wasn't. In Germany there were no grounds for one, just because Germany wasn't yet Germany. From Kant to Hölderlin to at least Hegel, the German philosophers understood themselves, in their own striking ways, to be operating in the absence of a revolution or in the expectation of another revolution, or to be in the process of ushering in a revolution that would be speculative rather than political. That's a phenomenon that has very often been commented on. And I think that it touches on something in thinking itself. It's as though, just because Germany hadn't yet been unified, while France had been for a long time (so long that now, I completely agree with you, it is faltering and suffering because it's too old), Germany developed in its thinking—with Fichte, Hegel, and so on—what it had not yet realized as a state. On the other hand, however, the French Revolution was in fact a philosophical operation. It involved the realization and putting into practice of a whole mode of thinking, while in Germany one felt at least partially powerless before the hypothesis of a revolution, or regarded it from a certain distance. I have to think of Kant here, who on the one hand extended his usual daily walk to receive news of the revolution and on the other declared that we do not have the right to strike down the sovereign.

So there is perhaps something important here, since it suggests that the Franco-German relationship has long been a philosophical relationship. And you're quite right, we would of course have to include England too, but then things would become very complicated, since what happens in England also plays a role in the politico-economic context in which this philosophical displacement takes place.

I don't want to go into a detailed analysis of that here—that's another question—but what I asked myself before this encounter was this: what key trait can I keep in mind where Germany is concerned? What did German philosophy essentially contribute when it so invigorated French thinking? I would say that there is perhaps something that emerges with (and only with) German philosophy—something that is already present yet barely visible in Kant, and becomes increasingly manifest in Hegel, Schelling, Hölderlin, and then Heidegger—namely, a preoccupation with the idea that the *saying* of philosophy, its enunciation, the mode of its enunciation—even its voice, if you like—should be present in what is said. If we take up the conceptual pair of the *saying* and the *said* here, without necessarily referring to Levinas, we can note that since Descartes and the ideologue philosophers of the revolutionary era, French philosophy has tended to take the form of a somewhat neutral mode of discourse and enunciation that manipulates objects. Germany, meanwhile, steeped thought in language from the outset. Leibniz was the first to declare that German was the best language in which to philosophize, but also that it wasn't yet mature enough. No French thinker ever said anything of the kind. And later we had Heidegger's statements on the advantages of German. I would say, then, that in this Franco-German relationship—you put this in a different way, but it overlaps with what I'm trying to say—the German element is more of a saying within the said, which also means that it's a philosophical discourse that is an act in itself, that is already something in its own right. That of course doesn't mean that it is praxis *tout court*, but that it itself is also a praxis. In that regard, there's someone you didn't mention, and that's Marx! Ah, you did it on purpose! Marx, incidentally, was perhaps the first almost Franco-Anglo-German philosopher. Or rather, in Marx there is both a grand discourse that manipulates objects and a voice that speaks, that wills, that wants to be heard and wants to let an appeal, a certain sensibility, ring out.

BADIOU   But Marx is so little German! Perhaps he's not exactly a philosopher, either. Anyway, let's leave Marx to one side.

VÖLKER   Jean-Luc, in discussing the question of revolution and idealism, you also mentioned Kant. I'd like to pursue this thread a little further. For you, Alain, it always seemed that Kant, as a philosopher of finitude, was a thinker who didn't rank particularly highly in your estimation. Yet one might think that the Kantian refutation of the existence of the whole, the distinction between knowledge and truth (as a distinction between the understanding and reason), and the conception of the Idea as a regulative Idea might all have exerted a significant influence on your work.

And for you, Jean-Luc, one might wonder in a very similar manner about the influence of the Kantian tradition. You wrote your dissertation on Kant, but later the names of Heidegger and Hegel feature more prominently in your work. And yet I've always wondered whether you would be prepared to describe a certain moment of rupture in the movement of being, a moment of interruption in every relation (which, as interruption, nonetheless belongs to being), as a Kantian point—including where movement as praxis is concerned.

BADIOU In truth, I don't like Kant. I admire him—he is extraordinarily tenacious and subtle—but admiring and liking aren't the same thing, especially in the terribly discontinuous field of great philosophical oeuvres. I don't like him much, first because I don't like the motif of the "limits of reason." Where the *Critique of Pure Reason* is concerned, I don't like the strictly critical aim, which is to determine the limits of pure reason, of cognitive rationality. I myself hold that reason, including the purest reason—mathematical reason, let's say—is absolutely without limit. Second, where the *Critique of Practical Reason* is concerned, I don't like the idea of the categorical imperative. I don't think that there is anything purely formal, like the categorical imperative, that would establish the universality of morality from the outset. I think there are of course imperatives, in the plural, that are tied to certain situations and events. But the scope of these imperatives, their matter and the subjectivity they require, is dependent on the worlds in which they hold sway. And where the *Critique of the Power of*

Judgment is concerned, I don't like the distinction between the beautiful and the sublime, which is the perfect symbol of the Romantic touch in all German Idealism.

One might then think that ultimately there's not a whole lot that I like in Kant, at least in the official Kant—the one reduced to a few slogans. And yet I feel continually compelled to enter into debate with him, to take up his terms again, to speak of the transcendental in my *Logics of Worlds*, for instance, and to often refer to various Kantian prefaces, introductions, and projects.

To be frank, I have an ambivalent relation to Kant, which I could summarize as follows: on the whole, he's a philosopher whose philosophical strategies don't appeal to me. In other words: I don't like *the critical project*. The idea that it's necessary to find a theoretically negative and practically sublime path between a supposed (Cartesian) "dogmatism" and a very real (Humean) empiricism doesn't fill me with enthusiasm. At the same time, I appreciate, of course, that Kant represents a kind of break, a transition, a new modernity, an admirable achievement. It makes me think of those people in our social circle whom we admire for their tenacity and subtlety, but whose obsessiveness makes them intolerable. That's essentially what I think of Kant—that he's the obsessive philosopher *par excellence*.

NANCY Except on the day he goes to fetch news of the revolution ...

BADIOU The one day! On that one day, marvel of marvels, Kant is hysterical. In any case, there are three kinds of

philosophers: the hysterics, the obsessives, and the para-
noiacs. And Kant is the greatest of the obsessives. I am
surely more paranoid: the absolute, the system, and so on.
But in spite of everything, Kant's grandeur is for me the
almost unbelievable grandeur of the obsessive. Kant is the
one who managed to turn his obsessions—his obsession
with the limit, his categorial obsession, his superegoic
obsession with the commandment, his obsession with the
subtle distinction between this and that, his invention of a
whole new esoteric vocabulary—into a new and indispens-
able philosophical oeuvre. But in everyday life such obsessions are intolerable. Imagine what it must have been like
to live with Kant!

NANCY No one did live with him, except his manservant!

BADIOU No one ever did—it would have been absolutely
impossible. But, you know, a philosopher no one can live
with is a problem! Perhaps he would advise everyone not to
live with anyone? With Descartes and Hegel, you have the
sense, even in the face of their most ambiguous conceptual
constructions, that you could spend a summer with them.
With Kant, it's out of the question. That's the bad side of
Kant's obsessive subjectivity. On the other hand, however,
beyond the obsessive constructions and the strategic the-
matics, there is the obstinate will and prideful modesty of a
professor who is both the agent of, and overwhelmed by, a
truly extraordinary ethics of inquiry.

But I realize I'm speaking of Kant somewhat inde-
pendently of the question of Germany here. For me, though,

the question of Germany—and earlier you indicated why—only emerges later on, because Germany itself only really emerges through a genuinely historical reflection on its own existence as an independent and unified state, as a world power. And this amounts to the invention of a historical Romanticism. Kant certainly approached this in his fit of enthusiasm for the sublimity of the French Revolution, but it isn't at the heart of his doctrine. It only begins a little later.

Now this question of the historically significant act—yes, you're right, that's the big question, up to and including Marx—this question of the philosopher's engagement, of the destiny of peoples, clearly also raises another big question, namely "What is Germany?" And the various responses to it more or less all amount to saying that Germany is the new Greece, that Germany is the homeland of thinking, that Germany is the site of philosophy—all of these nationalistic and megalomaniacal declarations. But at the same time they are indeed new, and they serve to introduce the question of history into philosophy. In doing so, they open up to universal thinking the continent of its historical destiny.

But Kant remains a particular case for me, one that precedes the Franco-German question and doesn't directly pose the problem of the historical, linguistic, and political frontiers of thinking. That's why I have an extremely ambivalent relation to him that I don't have to Hegel, whom I see as one of the three or four absolutely essential figures in the history of philosophy. For me, the history of the vital and concrete relation to German philosophy as such begins just after Kant.

NANCY I can agree with what you say about Kant not really being German—yes, he's Prussian first and foremost. Prussian and German, those are two different things, however important a role Prussia obviously played in the birth of Germany. But I completely disagree with everything else!

BADIOU I should hope so! Otherwise things are going to be very calm—too calm!

NANCY You say you don't like Kant. I understand, Kant isn't very likeable, he's not the most agreeable company. And that's also because he doesn't yet really write in German, but in what used to be called a chancellery language. He adores the old, stale Latin of the Middle Ages, he loves this scholastic language ... there are things in Latin in Kant that are absolutely exquisite, there's a kitsch side to him—but then Kant is fully aware of that. He is one of the very few philosophers to complain about not having the language he needs to expound his thinking. He wishes a poet could come along and do what he is unable to do. There's a passage in the third *Critique* where he discusses the possibility of a sublime work of art, and he indicates three possible forms that it could take: the didactic poem, the tragedy in verse, and the oratorio. And when he says "didactic poem," I'm almost certain he is thinking of Lucretius. Lucretius, incidentally, also inspired many other philosophers, as did the Platonic dialogue in its own way—Hegel, for example, states that we are no longer capable of writing dialogues like the Greeks because we no longer have their great models. So Kant is at least aware that his saying doesn't correspond sufficiently to what he wants to say.

So that's one thing. On the other hand, you say you don't like the limits of reason. But there I have to protest! Alain, there are no limits of reason for Kant! The limits of mere reason—the limits referred to in the title *Religion within the Limits of Reason Alone*—are the limits of a reason that rejects what Kant calls *Schwärmerei*—religious phantasmagoria. But aside from this project, in which Kant wanted to elaborate a religion that wouldn't fall into such a phantasmagoria, he is the first to admit that reason is impelled by a *Trieb*, that is, by what after Freud we would translate into French as *pulsion*, though for a long time it was translated as *instinct*. And what this pushes us toward is what Kant calls the unconditioned. But then—that's Badiou! *Warum nicht*? I don't know what you could object to there; you seem to me the victim of a rather too conventional reading of Kant, perhaps that of a certain Neo-Kantianism. For Kant, the limits of reason, that is, the principal object of the first *Critique*, reside in the delimitation of what he calls the understanding—*Verstand*—from reason. Now in the first *Critique*, one might of course have the impression that reason is simply being asked to abandon its claim to metaphysical knowledge. But you surely wouldn't be the one to oppose that? And so the self, the world, God—everything falls prey to critique. But what is

GERMAN PHILOSOPHY

the sense of this operation? For me, it is what opens up the whole of modernity, because it consists in saying: here it's no longer a question of an object of knowledge. I understand you might—recoil at that ...

BADIOU I'd certainly be uneasy!

NANCY But the fact that it's not a question here of objects of knowledge that would be presentable within the order of a knowledge of the object doesn't mean that all of Kant's subsequent work isn't already contained in the first *Critique*, in the resolution of the antinomies, and—or especially—in the two subsequent *Critiques*, particularly the third. All of Kant's further work lies in attempting to think what may be thinkable beyond the object, beyond what can be objectified by knowledge—what, I would say, is perhaps thought under the heading of the real. You didn't mention this but it's often thought that for Kant there are phenomena on the one hand and the thing-in-itself on the other, as though the thing-in-itself were hidden somewhere. Now I'm convinced—not by myself alone but also on the basis of the many readings of Kant that have appeared between his time and ours, not least Heidegger's—that the thing-in-itself is nothing other than the positing of the thing as such—the fact that it is posited, that it exists: it is existence. And when I reread Kant, even when I reread him through Badiou, if you will, I am also convinced that this positing of existence is multiple from the outset. There is no thing-in-itself somewhere behind our perception of phenomena. What there is, hanging from the ruins of the proof of the existence of God—which is nonetheless the cornerstone of the attack against a reason that indulges in fantasy—is the pure and simple existence of all things, an existence that is necessarily multiple. Somewhere in a posthumous fragment Kant asks how we can be sure that that isn't all just a dream. And the reason is simply that we can speak of it—it is there, the real exists [*il y a du reel*]. I don't want to exaggerate, but to exaggerate a little I'd almost say that Kant is the first existentialist. In essence, his whole operation—but here it's your critique that's pushing me to go further ...

BADIOU Be my guest!

NANCY I would say that it is Kant who, after the great period of classical rationalism—that is, Descartes, Spinoza, and Leibniz, and perhaps especially under the influence of the latter—raises the question, in an initial and obviously abstruse form, of a pure reality that is well and truly present and effective—a reality that we come up against and that pushes reason, according to its *Trieb*, to seek the unconditioned, the reason of all things, even though it knows it will not find it. It knows this because ultimately it can only find it in what Kant calls the keystone of the complete system of reason, namely, freedom. And freedom for Kant isn't simply the freedom of the classical free will: it is the freedom, as he says, to begin a new series of phenomena. It's also a freedom, then, that is bound up with history. So I was surprised when you said, "For me, Germany only emerges later on, with history," because history also emerges with Kant, in philosophy. He has a number of texts on the subject of history. So there you are, that's my Kant.

BADIOU   Well, that's some difference! But let me just say: What I think is that everything can be absolutely known. If you'll allow me to bring China into a Franco-German controversy, there's a nice expression of Mao's that goes: "We will come to know all that we did not know before." And Kant doesn't cease to explain why this is impossible. Even when he establishes a general principle of access to a real that is irreducible to the fiction of a hidden and inaccessible thing-in-itself, it's in a register that explicitly excludes knowledge—you can't pretend otherwise.

NANCY   Yes, he calls that *Glauben* ...

BADIOU   That's what I call—yes, the limits of the understanding, the limits of reason, the limits of rationality in general. And it's here that, in returning in reality to the classical, precritical field, I maintain the contrary thesis: ultimately, everything can be absolutely known.

NANCY   But you yourself sometimes speak of something—at least of a thing, if not the thing-in-itself—that you are convinced must exist, must be capable of existing, but that you do not know. You give it a name—you might call it communism or the possibility of a full and fulfilled existence, of the becoming existent of an inexistence ... I have some expressions in mind, but I don't have the texts here before me. I believe that's what you think! What is Badiou's "I believe"?

BADIOU I believe that everything *can* be absolutely known! Your objection that I know there are many things that we don't yet know is no real objection. I don't claim that we do know absolutely everything. I claim that the axiom of knowledge as such is that we can know everything. There is the not known and the unknown, but strictly speaking there's nothing unknowable.

NANCY What does "know" mean?

BADIOU Well, as my master, Plato, would say, that would be a long digression ...

NANCY But we've got time ...

BADIOU OK, let's take the canonical example of Kant's being-in-itself. From this point on, all of the sciences converge on the idea that this being-in-itself, that is, being thought in the pure objective dimension of its being as such, is nothing other than the general system of the possible forms of multiplicity. Now this system of the possible forms of multiplicity is one we can explore mathematically and thereby come to know. Whatever question you ask me, I will give you the *register* of the possible knowledge of it.

I'm not at all saying that this knowledge has unfolded fully, that it has reached a state of absoluteness, if we understand absoluteness as the Whole. But it is always possible. As soon as we start to say that there is a "thing" whose true nature is that we cannot know it, we enter the realm of obscurantism—we adopt a dangerous vision of existence according to which we have to accommodate and live with things that exist, that are there, but that we can neither know nor even understand.

Now I think this kind of vision manifests itself in all sorts of contemporary claims. When the prime minister of my country says that to attempt to explain something is already to justify it (yes, he said it in relation to the mass murders in Paris last November), then this amounts to saying: if you attempt to explain these terrible things, you are already on the way to excusing them. He said: to explain, that is, to attempt to know, to understand, is already to excuse. And that's a very widespread idea. Combatting this idea philosophically requires us to affirm that this kind of statement is obscurantist and inadmissible. We have to universally uphold the thesis that we can acquire genuine knowledge of what takes place. Kant, just like English empiricism, can be enlisted in support of the contrary thesis, namely that there are strict limits to our cognitive capacities, and that the unknowable therefore exists. Now, of course, one can also read Kant in other ways, if one sets out from the concept of practical reason. But one can't ignore the fact that he can be used, on a common reading of "critical" thought, to support the thesis that the unknowable really exists and that this unknowable is all the more important insofar as it coincides with the being-in-itself of all that exists.

NANCY   But even for Kant it's not a question of speaking of the unknowable, but of the unknowable in the mode of the construction of an object, of an object produced by an experimental operation upon matter, according to the Galilean and Newtonian model, as you know. And it's from this kind of knowledge that Kant wishes to exclude absolutely the metaphysical objects of God, the immortal self, and the world as totality. So in no way does he say that these things are unknowable; he rather says that it's a question here of another kind of knowledge. Now, of course, he doesn't put it that way, but ultimately he says that it's a question of a different kind of relation between reason and its objects. And on the one hand, this relation—still in Kant's terms, though I won't say that I'll always want to stick to them—takes the form of the second *Critique*, that is, of the categorical imperative that you don't like, even though the categorical imperative is nothing other than reason enjoining itself to infinitely transform things as they are, in such a way that every action could be thought as a universal law of nature. For Kant, this is to put oneself in the position of God without God. In the third *Critique*, on the other hand, it's a question of thinking ends—always called final ends—as though we could indeed think them as ends, even though we know—and that really is something we know!—that they are not ends. Why? Because the human being is the being of ends. So that's a long way from simply saying: there is the known on the one hand and the unknowable on the other.

VÖLKER Let me take up the role of *agent provocateur* again. Following this discussion of limits, in which we've also touched on the notion of totality, and since Hegel's name in a certain sense goes hand in hand with Kant's: Hegel is for both of you a crucial figure. The question I'd like to ask you here is this: How much system is necessary to think negativity? The "restlessness of the negative," to cite one of Jean-Luc's works (which itself cites an expression of Hegel's), is for you, Alain, still rooted in the One of the Hegelian system. Is that then the Hegelian question—the question of whether negativity can only be thought within the One of a system? That it must be? That it cannot be?

NANCY Hegel is negativity as movement—the movement, as he says, through which the One is its own negation or through which being, understood as the "spiritless copula," immediately sublates itself. In a certain sense, this is something extremely simple—almost nothing—but in this nothing there is a mobility, an activity, that Hegel reproaches Kant for lacking. As he says in *Faith and Knowledge*, Kant has erected an admirable statue, but since it has no blood in its veins it cannot but crumble. For me, then, Hegelian negativity is movement. It's much less the movement of a system, even though there is a system. I have nothing against the system, but here I again have to cite Kant, who says that systems are living beings that develop and intersect with one another. I agree: there is no thinking that is not systematic, that is, that does not form a whole. What would that mean—a thinking made up of fragments? But for all that, a system isn't an imposing edifice. I understand that, for you, it's an edifice that proceeds from principles and allows us to subject everything to these principles. For me, by contrast, Hegel is equally, not exactly the antisystem, but—I'm not sure what to call it—the hypersystem? The hypersystem that does not cease to systematize itself. As soon as one starts to speak of Hegel, what inevitably comes to mind is the last page of the *Phenomenology of Spirit*, with its (modified) citation from Schiller: "*Aus dem Kelche dieses Geisterreiches schäumt ihm seine Unendlichkeit* [From the chalice of this realm of spirits foams forth for Him his own infinitude]." *Gibt es nicht darin auch ein bißchen Badiou*? The *Phenomenology*'s last word is a foaming forth, not from "Him" but from this chalice. There is a totality here, but a totality that proves the totality is not at all a closed totality, but rather one that foams forth to itself as its own infinity.

Furthermore, it's certainly true that Hegel played an important role for me in my studies, since through one of those chance meetings or contingencies, I once encountered someone who taught Hegel in France with great passion. And finally, let me add that Hegel represents for me, along with Schelling, and perhaps some others, something that I think is very much lacking in contemporary philosophy and that was known in that era as *Naturphilosophie*—the philosophy of nature. Of course, the idea of a philosophy of nature seems a little ridiculous today. Hegel, for example, gives us the meaning of everything—of all the elements—and explains what light is, what a solid is, a gas, a mineral, a vegetable, a living being, and so on. But such *Naturphilosophie* is also a way of giving voice to all things or traversing all things through language [*parole*], and that seems to me something that philosophy wishes to do, must do, and tries to do. So there are these two things, then: movement and giving voice to everything.

BADIOU I would first like to say that I only have a really passionate relation to three philosophers: Plato, Descartes, and Hegel. For me, that's the systematic concentrate of the history of philosophy. And my relation to Hegel is the complete opposite of my relation to Kant. I like Hegel, really. I like him even in all his moments of madness that you mentioned. He even tried to deduce the exact number of planets as an attribute of the absolute. That was a big risk, which was immediately rewarded by the discovery of an extra planet. Normally, you would expect that to cause the collapse of the whole system, because there are no purely local parts in the Hegelian system; there is a general interlinking of these parts, and if Hegel was wrong about the number of planets, he was perhaps wrong about many other things, too. But at the end of the day, I like all of that—I like it for the reasons you gave. Because I approve of this movement whereby philosophy traverses all things through what you call, a little too generally, "language"— that's also how I see things. But however much I love Hegel, what stops me from really being at home in Hegel's thinking, from being at ease there, is his frenetic desire for exhaustion, the impatient passion of the encyclopedist, the desire to show that we are already—or at least that he is already—at the point of acceding to the totality of all possible shapes of consciousness, for example, without leaving any real space for the indetermination of what is to come. Hegel seeks to exhaust every shape of subjectivity between immediate sensibility and absolute knowledge. And as you said, it's the same for nature—the idea of an exhaustion of its determinations. So I have the sense of a closure that insinuates itself into the heart of the dispersive and creative process of negativity—not exactly in the form of a pregiven totality, but rather in that of an integral fulfillment, a completed pathway. Yes, Hegel really does think that philosophy is a completed pathway. At the end of the day, the absolute is with us from the outset, and Hegel is able to present the various stages on the long march through which it subjectivizes itself, in order ultimately to absorb this very path in the mode of a conscious new beginning [*recommencement*]. As Hegel himself puts it in an extraordinary formulation, the absolute ultimately absolves itself of its own absoluteness. And yet, one still has the impression that this final absolution leaves intact the fact that we have passed through all possible forms of subjectivation. And so I think that despite all the objections one might raise to this totalizing vision, there is the sense of an end in Hegel, in both senses of the term: the end is both the ultimate destiny of the shapes of consciousness in the space of possibility of absolute knowledge and the eventual renunciation of the previous stages. If we take art, for example, the idea of the end of art cannot be interpreted as the end of all artistic activity—it's not that at all—but rather as the end of the necessity of art for the unfolding of spirit. Since the end of Greek art, in fact, its status as a historical figure of the absolute has been exhausted. And it's on that basis that Hegel can say that art is a thing of the past. It's here we reach the limit of my Hegelian interiority, which is nonetheless very expansive.

As for the rest, the movement of negativity, Hegel's extraordinary sense of the transition from one thing to another, his incredible reading of history, which he describes in the manner of a brilliant novel, holding us in suspense at each stage, introducing dramatic turns of events within a seemingly global process of determination, while also making monumental errors (which are ultimately unimportant) and showing a poorly justified sovereign contempt (which one can nonetheless overlook)—all of that has a considerable conceptual beauty. And here I would agree with what you said: it's true that there is a fascinating form of commitment in his prosodic constructions themselves—one that is surely a Hegelian invention, with a quasi-aesthetic character and an authentic linguistic power that never shrinks from the most extravagant jargon. Hegel's language is a constant treasure trove—and the best proof of this is that whenever we try to translate him we end up falling back on his German terms.

For all these reasons, Hegel represents an important horizon for me, since he is the true thinker of negativity—not the morose, negative negativity of Adorno, but an affirmative and creative negativity. Hegel is a great inventor, a dynamic thinker—conceptual in an intense, effervescent, surprising, and somewhat jargon-heavy manner, but endowed with real genius. And that's why he seems to be our contemporary—aside from the idea of the exhaustion of both the real and the possible, which in my view isn't very contemporary.

NANCY First of all, it is important to note, whether we are talking of Kant or of Hegel, that we cannot relate to them as we do to our contemporaries. We necessarily come after them, and we reread them. What strikes me is that you say, "I don't like Kant, I like Hegel," whereas what I say of the one or the other isn't primarily a question of affect, but of a reception. I know that what I say is mediated by various readings; I wouldn't have the relation to Hegel that I do without Kojève—or, going beyond Kojève, without Bataille, or many others, including Derrida. So first of all, we are not doing our shopping in the philosophical supermarket; we are who we are now, in 2016, and so we take up various perspectives and try out various ways of seeing what has taken place and what has given rise to us.

Second: exhaustion. Here I'm not so sure, because absolute knowledge is nothing other than spirit's journey back through all of its various shapes. And Hegel doesn't claim that all of these are complete in his time. He does of course think that there is something in the process of coming to fulfillment, and he sees this fulfillment very much in the figure of the state. Indeed, he sees in the state a double fulfillment, one of which I think is very keenly observed: Hegel is namely the first to show that the state not only amounts to the administration of civil society but also to what he calls the *sittliche Idee*. That doesn't mean the "moral" idea—though I believe it's translated into French as *l'idée morale*—but rather the ethical idea in action. And through a historical representation that is of its time, this ethical idea in action takes the form of a constitutional monarch. Thanks to the dynastic principle, the monarch materially incarnates the idea through his contingent and natural person alone (Hegel insists on this), while doing no more than signing his name. Yet behind this monarchical signature lies the mystery of what Hegel calls the ethical Idea. Only philosophy, he says, is in a position to contemplate this majesty. Now you could, of course, construe that as an expression of a certain exhaustion, but in reality it signifies that for Hegel true politics is the superpolitics or hyperpolitics of philosophy, and one might say that that opens just as well onto the disappearance of the state in favor of something that would more fully embody the ethical idea in action. What I mean is that in Hegel there is something that is always in the process of disturbing the possibility of exhaustion, such as contingency. The person of the monarch is contingent, and elsewhere in Hegel there are further examples of the indisputable character of contingency. There is a section in the *Encyclopaedia* where he attacks someone, whose name I forget, saying, "so-and-so wants me to deduce the necessity of the pen with which I'm writing, it's absolutely ridiculous, etc." So whether it's a question of the monarch or my pen, not everything can be deduced and everything doesn't lead to an exhaustive system. I won't say that there isn't also a tendency toward exhaustion. But Hegel not only leads to the foaming forth at the end of the *Phenomenology*, but also to the end of the *Encyclopaedia*, where, citing Aristotle, he says that spirit enjoys itself. Indeed, Hegel is perhaps the first thinker of infinite *jouissance*,* and as it happens, he belongs to an age marked by a kind of release. Hegel follows Spinoza, with whom he shares a great deal, even if in Spinoza it's called *joy* (a word that is nonetheless the doublet of *jouissance*). Now *jouissance* in Hegel—and it's no coincidence that there's a connection with foam here—is precisely that which cannot cease, that which cannot exhaust itself. You speak of that which comes to an end, that which is cut off, in a text where you criticize me for thinking, as you put it, "a *jouissance* ... of the angels"—and you add, "but be careful, it does end all the same." I don't disagree: infinite *jouissance* is finite. The finite opens itself infinitely. I would say that the *jouissance* of which Hegel speaks is his way of naming the relation to the outside of a spirit—to use his terms—that precisely cannot exhaust itself by itself, that cannot arrive at its own end. But to be unable to arrive at one's own end is at the same time to be infinitely fulfilled.

*[As Jean-Luc Nancy himself notes in his preface to Charlotte Mandell's translation of his *La Jouissance*, the latter term "designates the entire, limitless usage of a possession, with the twofold connotation of appropriation (or *consummation*, consumption) and pleasure carried to its height" (Jean-Luc Nancy and Adèle Van Reeth, *Coming*, trans. Charlotte Mandell [New York: Fordham University Press, 2017], viii). Since both of these connotations play an important role in the following dialogue, I have chosen to leave the noun *jouissance* untranslated, while using "to enjoy" as a translation of the verb *jouir*—Trans.]

And what is infinite fulfillment? That's the question I would put to you.

BADIOU But this infinite fulfillment is directly related to the fact that the absolute is nothing but the subject of its own pathway. So the infinite in Hegel is the pathway itself insofar as it is subjectivized. And none of that can be contained within a substantial delimitation. The foam is simply the fact that spirit, having arrived at absolute knowledge, is now in a position to contemplate and breathe life into the totality of its shapes *in their subjectivized dimension*. To be sure, nothing is "complete" in the sense of a closure that would prevent any further examination; but there is still an exhaustion of possibilities.

Aside from that, I'd also like to make a methodological remark concerning reading. My reading of authors, of philosophical constructors, is much more naïve than yours. I take very seriously what they themselves say about what they are doing. You say that successive interpretations modify all that. But no, they don't modify philosophers' explicit assertions about what their project really is. You can't deny, even if you would rather it weren't true, that Hegel's project consists in an exhaustion of all historical possibilities. You can't deny that the absolute is the subjectivized recollection of those "shapes" that make up its pathway. You can't deny—and as it happens you just said it—that Hegel sees in Prussian bureaucracy the definitive, absolute figure of the state, and so on. Now as I see it, that's all part of the necessary *singularity* of individual philosophers. It's an internal testament to the fact that all their strength, all their grandeur, lies in their capacity to extract from a historical material as determined as it is precarious a certain measure of universality. The grandeur of these philosophers would be less manifest if we "corrected" or erased the innumerable traces of contingency in their works. There's no need to correct anything whatsoever.

NANCY   There's no need to, but we can't do otherwise! Just because there is history and because we come afterward. I completely agree with you, we have to know what we want to do—if we really want to read Hegel, we have to know why we want to read Hegel, because we're not obliged to reread him the whole time. But if we really want to read Hegel and really establish what is contained in Hegel, then you are absolutely right. But that also means that we have to consider Hegel in the context of his own time—in just the time I was speaking of earlier, a time in which Germany wasn't yet in the process of modernizing its state, as France was. So that's one thing. But today, in any case, we can hardly purport to read Hegel as though we were living at the turn of the nineteenth century.

BADIOU   But that's not at all what I mean to do! I want to read Hegel naïvely *as a naïve reader today*, and to make of him what I will—that's all. That's my position in relation to the great philosophers. At a push, I'd gladly do for all of them what I did for Plato, that is, rewrite them.

NANCY   But just look, it doesn't bother you to say, ultimately, "I take what is in Plato and I rewrite it wholly otherwise." Well, that's something else again …

BADIOU   Yes, I rewrite it otherwise on the basis of what I call an effective and naïve reading of what, as I see it, he has said in the Greek text I read. It's by no means a sophisticated hermeneutic that would consist in saying: ultimately, what Hegel perhaps really wanted to say ... or, there that's not really how it is ... or, we now know, thanks to X's reading, that Hegel is not at all what we always thought he was ... or, we know that this naïve reading of Hegel, which was perhaps also his own, is untenable ... In fact, every time I attack him, you play Hegel's advocate—and Kant's too—saying, "My dear boy, these attacks are quite unjustified, since if he says that, it's because of his time; in truth, if he had known, he would have said something else." You modernize him too, but in order to defend him.

NANCY   Yes, I modernize him, but not in order to say, "This is what he was really or truly saying"; no, I say, "Here is what now, after a certain number of ..."

BADIOU   All the same, you did say, "What he perhaps said ..."

NANCY   OK, everyone has their moments of weakness. I am guided by the sentiment, and more than just the sentiment, that there is a continuous movement—the movement of history—which, as you said, resulted in various exchanges and intersections between France and Germany, and other countries too. All of that is what makes up history. Now Marx—earlier on I understood you wanted us to exclude him from the debate, but I'll insist a little all the same—Marx says that philosophers don't spring from the earth like mushrooms. So you're not a mushroom, I'm not a mushroom, it's not even certain that we're philosophers … no, it is, let's admit it. And philosophers—like artists and scholars and everyone else—are products of their time. What is "their time"? It is a particular moment—there are temporal rhythms, and so there are certain moments when something takes on a certain form.

BADIOU So they are indeed mushrooms! Complicated mushrooms!

NANCY If you like. I've often thought that, because Marx is a little mistaken here—he seems to think that mushrooms arise through a kind of spontaneous generation …

BADIOU And you are restoring the truth of the mushroom …

NANCY Whereas in fact, mushrooms only grow in certain places. It's well known that porcini mushrooms, for example, don't grow just anywhere. Mushrooms grow under certain conditions, including those of light, humidity, and so on. To that extent, Marx is mistaken, and it would be better to say something like, "philosophers don't fall from the sky." The question is then: if philosophy too isn't just a succession of singularities that happened to arise—why Kant and why Hegel? Well, Kant emerged because a critical moment had arrived—one marked by a range of things, including *Sturm und Drang* in Germany and Rousseau in France—and in this critical moment it was a question of shaking up the dominant systems of the representation of reason. And Hegel ... well, that's another story.

Philosophers are then produced by their time *and* produced by their time with the task of thinking their time. That's precisely what Hegel himself says—that philosophy comes along when a form of life is drawing to a close—but what's interesting is that Hegel says that philosophy then paints its gray on gray, so ultimately this whole affair is quite sad. It's sad for Hegel because, as he says elsewhere in the *Aesthetics*, our (i.e., his) time is bereft of the colors of life. He is then already the first thinker of a form of ... I wouldn't say decline, that would be going too far where Hegel is concerned, but, if you like, of exhaustion, since the exhaustion you spoke of is also the sense that something is coming to an end or entering a state of suspension. And gray is the absence of color. In truth, Hegel would like to see more colors around him. Every philosopher is also a symptom. So, you reproach me for modernizing, but that's not what I do—it's rather that I am able, by way of Heidegger and Derrida, to draw out certain threads in Hegel that he himself didn't draw out, and that are also not those that Kojève felt he could draw out.

VÖLKER One name that has mainly been present through its absence so far is that of Marx. Jean-Luc, you once described Marx as a powerful machine, one that managed to measure the whole field of its epoch, while also showing how capitalism produces its own transgression in the form of *jouissance*. And for you, Alain, Marxism (rather than Marx) is essential for the second sequence of the communist hypothesis, but you have also said that we are now in a similar situation to Marx before he wrote the *Manifesto*. From a philosophical and contemporary perspective, then, to what extent is the practical difference that Marx introduced into philosophy lacking today? The question would then concern the absence of Marx. Or does Marx rather denote a difference internal to philosophy?

BADIOU Yes, for me it's difficult to describe Marx straightforwardly as a philosopher. To be honest, I have the same difficulty with Freud. And I think that in both cases it's tied to the fact that their thinking is explicitly oriented toward a definite praxis. Not "praxis in general," which after all is a concept, but a definite praxis. Marx uses philosophical links or philosophical sources, but his aim is in no way to produce a philosophical oeuvre. It is rather to participate in the class struggle of his time, to draw the appropriate lessons from the failure of the revolutions of the 1840s, and to establish and guide a workers' international, all on the basis of a critique of political economy. Furthermore, it's well known that Marx gives a critique of philosophy in general. Thus far, he says, philosophers have only interpreted the world, whereas the point is to change it. As he sees it, this requires a rupture. Now, it seems to me that—whether it's a question of a communist international and all the associated revolutionary practices or the psychoanalytic profession and the definition of a cure—in all such cases where philosophy is enlisted solely in order to contribute to the constitution, the creation, of a singular, organized, and codified praxis, we need to invent a particular designation. Because strictly speaking, there is no philosophical praxis. Neither revolution nor psychoanalytic cures can be described as philosophical practices. They are practices that perhaps incorporate philosophical elements, but they are not philosophical practices. In truth, the existence of philosophy, like the existence of art, is nothing but the manifestation of great singular oeuvres tied to proper names. And a philosopher is someone who creates a philosophical oeuvre that stands the test of time. So I would prefer to say that there is philosophy in Marx, without thereby being forced to say that Marx is a philosopher. And that means that there is always something difficult in philosophical discussions on Marx, because they can't be conducted like those on Hegel, Kant, or Descartes, for instance, or even Plato. I would say the same about Freud or Lacan, or Lenin or Mao. In all of these remarkable thinkers, the philosophical ingredients are put in the service of a singular, rigorously defined end, which in itself is extraphilosophical.

Now we can, of course, ask how we should then treat the judgments that Marx or Lacan make about philosophy. And to be honest, I think the first part of Marx's famous dictum in the "Theses on Feuerbach" is simply inexact. To say that philosophers have only "interpreted the world" doesn't do any real justice to philosophy. Philosophy's conceptual work manifests itself as something other than an interpretation of the world. It may intersect with this kind of task, but it cannot be reduced to it. The interpretation of the world rather constitutes the essence of myths, religions, wisdoms, and the like. Philosophy, essentially rational and based on the sciences—especially mathematics—is thus conceptual rather than hermeneutic. Philosophy is a system of singular questions, at the center of which lies, in my view, the following question: Does there exist anything with a universal value—and if so, how is this possible? Other philosophers would put this question differently, but they all articulate singular questions that by no means amount to "interpretations" of the world. It's true, then, that philosophers don't put forward a program to transform the world, in the political sense. They might touch on this kind of activity, but it's not their real aim, no more than it is to offer an interpretation of the world. So the idea of moving from interpretation to change seems to me to miss the mark. Why? Because it's a judgment made within the context of a political polemic, in which Marx is settling accounts with the old, rabidly conservative Hegelians on the one hand and Feuerbach, who lacks an analysis of class, on the other.

To sum up, then, I would emphasize two points: One, Marx isn't strictly speaking a philosopher, even though he makes use of philosophy; two, the judgment that he passes on philosophy and that would seem to produce a radical break within it (this was to some extent Althusser's interpretation) is a judgment that does not seem to me very pertinent and in reality didn't produce any radical break in the history of philosophy.

NANCY I can only agree with what you said last. But I interpret everything else you said very differently. I agree that whatever definition we might give of philosophy, Marx isn't really a philosopher. But I would add a little more ... not more than you, but I would say that Marx isn't a philosopher because he doesn't do what every other philosopher does— he doesn't go as far as he possibly can, with the means at his disposal, in his attempt to pose, to say, to name, to designate what he doesn't cease to consider as the end of action. He doesn't name what he is striving for, even if it is unnamable. For me, there are two key examples of this. The first is his famous statement that religion is the spirit of a world without spirit. It's a brilliant statement, and very effective against religion, but not enough attention is paid to the fact that, if he says this world is without spirit, then that must mean he is familiar with something that goes by the name of "spirit" and he observes that it isn't here. But at no point does he say, "I shall now attempt to say what spirit is." And it's the same with the statement, which I believe appears twice in his works, that the point is not to establish collective property (as has so often been assumed), but rather that the disappearance of private property would also bring about the disappearance of collective property and allow individual property to appear. Now Marx names individual property here but he says nothing about it. And it's because he doesn't say what individual property is that he's not a philosopher.

So we can agree on that. But at the same time, if we go back a little before *Capital*, if we return to the manuscripts of 1844, without worrying about Althusser's epistemological break, we can nonetheless find certain elements that help us to think what an individual might be. I recently reread a passage from the 1844 manuscripts, for example, where Marx speaks of the *jouissance* of the worker, the producer, at gaining recognition through his work and his production—in and through his work. Here we can already glimpse a small element of what he understands by an individual. And what he understands by an individual is very, very far from what we would call an individual today—who knows, perhaps he even conceives a subject who could just as well be collective. In any case, he conceives a *jouissance*—a *jouissance* of one's own value, recognized as such. And at that moment, *jouissance*—that's his word, *Genuß*, *genießen*—this *jouissance* takes on the sense or the value of the self-evaluation of a value. And a value that evaluates itself is a value that has no need of evaluation: it's a value that is absolutely valuable by itself. Here and there, I have tried to show that all of Marx rests on the thinking of an absolute value, and that this absolute value is called "humanity" insofar as each of us is both the producer of our existence and a social or collective producer. But Marx doesn't even develop that idea; he perhaps doesn't have the means to do so, though it does resonate in certain of his images that remain with us today. As he describes it in *The Holy Family* or *The German Ideology*, as you know, the worker liberated from his alienating wage-labor will work in the morning, go fishing in the afternoon, and play the violin in the evening. Now here there is something that even doubles *jouissance*, since working in the morning would already afford me recognition as a producer, while fishing would … well, I'm not sure exactly what kind of recognition it would bring, I'm not enough of an angler for that ... and the violin, well, that's clear. So in Marx, as I read him, there is something of the order of the enjoyment of an absolute value. To that extent, I wouldn't say that he's not a philosopher; I would say he is a philosopher who stopped at a certain point, or perhaps that he is a philosopher who let himself get caught up in an urgent task, and after all we're not going to reproach him for that. In that sense, Marx did far more than just protest against the abominable conditions of labor and commodity production. He also put his finger—a philosophical finger, what else?—on something that was very much coming to a head. I would say that that wasn't simply the death of God, but the death of the *jouissance* of value. Perhaps there is also a link between God and *jouissance*, but let's leave that to one side. To that extent, then, I would say he is a philosopher who did indeed do a lot of good for philosophy.

BADIOU I agree with you there. He used philosophy in a way that was useful for it. But I'd just like to add that there is something in the manuscripts of 1844 that is decisive for me, namely the idea that the aspect of humanity that comes to the fore in Marx's historical era (which to a certain extent is also our era) is what he calls *generic humanity*. And generic humanity is very much a philosophical category. The whole problem is to identify, in existing societies, the trace, the recognizable figure, of this generic humanity. This is linked to the idea that human activity itself ought to be generic rather than specialized—to the critique of the division of labor you mentioned, on the basis of the idea that every individual should become a polymorphous worker—and to the very important notion of the end of the opposition between intellectual and manual workers. There is a whole Marxist anthropology on the future of the value of humanity as such, a value conditional on what we might define as the generic dimension of humanity. I completely agree with you: all of that was only sketched in Marx's works. And the fact that it remained so resulted in a sort of ungainliness in his handling of the critical opposition between scientific and utopian communism. Please note, everyone, that it's on Marx that Jean-Luc and I have found some points of agreement. That's a symptom indeed!

NANCY In what you said about Marx, there was also another point, namely that philosophy isn't an interpretation of the world. I completely agree with you on that, but I would define it differently. Let me say two things here: first, when you say that philosophy isn't an interpretation of the world, isn't that rather close to what Heidegger says in relation to the *Weltbilder*—the images of the world, the "age of the world picture"? I wonder whether there isn't a certain proximity between you there—the obviously enormous difference being that, for Heidegger, the age of the world picture precisely brings to a close what he calls philosophy, whose end he declares in order to speak of a thinking that would be still to come. For you, however, to say that philosophy isn't an interpretation of the world is to regain the whole of philosophy, to preserve its name and its character as the persistent, meticulous, and attentive posing of the question, "Is there a universal value?" But what I'd like to ask you, even if it disrupts the order of these questions a little, is this: Why did philosophy begin?

BADIOU   You're asking me?

NANCY   Yes, I'm asking you!

BADIOU   You're right to ask me, because I know very well why it began. Philosophy began because mathematics began.

NANCY   Why did mathematics begin?

BADIOU   That I can't tell you. If I could tell you why mathematics began, I would be in a position to give an exhaustive account of the evental figures through which humanity arrives at its generic figure, that is, its absoluteness. The beginning of mathematics is an event, which has a historical [*historiale*] dimension. That's the reason why every attempt to explain this event, like any other event worthy of the name, is doomed to failure. Why? Because an event is an immanent exception to the laws of a given situation. So you can make all the anthropological speculations you want, I know them by heart: there are the Egyptian preconditions, the Babylonian preconditions; mathematics could only have emerged in the Greek anthropological or political context, and so on. Ultimately, that helps us circumscribe the thing itself a little better, but no one is able to say *why*— in the radical sense—mathematics emerged at that very moment and in that very place.

NANCY Sure, but I'm not asking "why in the radical sense," but just a regular "why." Because, as you said, there are the Egyptians, the Babylonians, and all of these factors, and then at a certain moment there is mathematics as such. Everyone agrees on that. The question is rather, "Why was there such an enormous change?" And here it's not enough just to say "on account of the Greek anthropological context." Because Greece itself represents the birth of mathematics, philosophy, politics, but this birth takes place because a world has changed.

BADIOU Clearly. But since you can't distinguish between the *fact* that a world has changed and the nature of the change in this world, we fall back on the eventual. So I'll ask you why the world changed at that very moment.

NANCY And I'm going to tell you.

BADIOU You're going to tell me ...

NANCY Because the gods departed. You speak of Egypt, you speak of Babylon; you might well speak of everything that came before that. You speak of a still-theocratic whole, and there were several forms of it. That brings to mind Braudel's remark that everything before the ninth century BC is obscure for the historian. But this obscurity is now beginning to dissipate a little, and we know a little more about the great whirlwind that swept through the Mediterranean at the end of the Bronze Age and the beginning of the Iron Age. Now I'm very mindful of the fact that, as Hegel puts it, there are first myths, naïveté, and so on, and then finally reason appears. And today we are still beholden to this miraculous birth of reason, which for you is represented by the matheme in all its Greek splendor. Yet here you take the Greek precisely as already given—as given all at once—whereas I'm always haunted by the fact that there are first of all a certain number of conditions at work—techniques, practices, navigation, arithmetic ... Now Babylonian arithmetic certainly isn't mathematics as we would understand it, but it is already a lot—and the same goes for the arithmetic and land-surveying methods of the Egyptians, alphabetic writing, and so on. These are all important elements in the complete transformation of civilization. In a word, then, in this part of the world, in this rather Oriental Mediterranean region, there suddenly emerges a humanity that goes about transforming generic humanity. There is a humanity to whom it is no longer given, and here I won't even name what it is that's no longer given—sense, truth, whatever you will—it's no longer given. And then we see the birth of mathematics, politics, and philosophy. And we mustn't forget ...

BADIOU   Tragedy ...

NANCY   These are all various attempts to give oneself or to acquire something where it isn't given. Oh, but you agree with that?

BADIOU   Absolutely.

NANCY: Yes, but it's not a miraculous birth!

BADIOU I didn't say it was a miracle. But you haven't given the least explanation of it either!

NANCY No—I'm not saying I'm going to explain it. I'm only asking that philosophy look over its shoulder a little. Because I think we shouldn't cease to reflect—if not as an explication—on the fact that at a certain moment the given world (which, I forgot to mention, also included human sacrifice) came to an end—and from this moment on, from this event, which was in itself multiple, there emerged what we know today as civilization.

BADIOU I completely agree. I have always insisted that mathematics is only ever the most radical and concentrated form of a far more general phenomenon, namely, that what it is to speak the truth is no longer a question of a prescribed enunciative position. What we and the classicists call "Greece" is the moment when the validity of a statement is no longer seen as organically tied to the person making it. So with "Greece" we enter an era in which, if you want to maintain the universal truth of a statement, you have to put it up for discussion among everyone who understands its meaning. Mathematics is simply the encoding, at a total level of abstraction that I consider the ontological level, of this phenomenon that we both acknowledge—this profound upheaval. At this point, we leave behind a world where the legitimacy, the validity, of what is said depends on the person who says it (and where this ultimately leads back to an interpreter of the gods, a prophet, a king, an established authority). What appears with "Greece" is something like the nudity of truth. From now on, one has to argue; if one defends a thesis, if one holds an opinion, one has to argue. Likewise if one rejects a thesis or challenges an opinion. And politics itself then comes to be situated within this element, since it's necessary to argue for the statements one makes at the democratic citizens' assembly. I agree with you about the nature of this general shift. And when you say, "Suddenly, something is no longer given," I completely agree with your formulation. Mathematics simply amounts to the written, abstract, radical testing of this point: a proof is a proof, and if someone claims to have proved something, then he or she has to write this proof down and discuss it with his or her colleagues. And then we'll see if it's true or not. That's what "Greece" is. I agree with you there. But you didn't explain it, you didn't say where it came from, and why there and not somewhere else, and why sometime around the fifth century BC. You merely said that that's what it was.

NANCY   Agreed. But that's already something, since we have already advanced a little if we can say "It's that." But it also seems to me that the whole endeavor to give oneself what is no longer given, that is, the endeavor to speak the truth, to achieve verification, is accompanied by a diffuse sentiment that I don't know how to name but that perhaps also derives from the experience of loss, of the absence of something—to such an extent that even in our time the fact that it isn't given continues to trouble us. But it seems to me that in pointing to the possibility, and not only the possibility, of the impossible (since ultimately one could summarize the orientation of your thought in that way), you compensate, as Mallarmé says, for the lack of a point of departure. And if this point of departure lies in the subtraction of the given, if this point of departure—which it truly is, and which for us has withdrawn, absolutely, indefinitely, insofar as God or the gods are really dead—then it's not Nietzsche, nor Jean Paul, nor Luther who invented that: there were already Greeks who said "The gods have departed." And even in Plato—Plato names *theos* in the singular, at least in the *Theaetetus*, where it's said that one should flee toward the *theos* (which was translated by the Jesuits as "God," while the secular translators opted for "god," and more recent translators "the divine"). What I mean is that, with the advent of this anonymous or metaphoric *theos*, the gods have already vanished.

BADIOU Since the Greeks, I think that the gods, in many different manifestations, haven't ceased to die—and to rise again, here and there.

NANCY But if they really have risen again, there have also been many false resurrections. But doesn't that also mean that the task of philosophy cannot simply be to rediscover or reach a point where "it" will be given again? "It" being the truth. Because we could then know it (anew) in its entirety as given? Or because it—the true—would begin to be given again?

BADIOU I think that the task of philosophy is to find rational and shareable protocols so that humanity isn't poisoned by its mourning of the death of the gods.

NANCY   Because Buddha's shadow remains before his cave for a thousand years, as Nietzsche says?

BADIOU   Exactly. But the point is not to try to make up for the loss, but rather to habituate humanity as a whole to the fact that its own creative constitution lies in the element of this loss—and that's not the same thing. Philosophy, as I see it, amounts to the organization of a mourning that genuinely paves the way for forgetting by establishing itself in loss as in the natural element of its own existence. The genuinely creative element is one in which a shared and shareable universality is possible, precisely because the gods are all dead. That's what Wagner clearly saw at the end of the *Götterdämmerung*: the total failure, on both sides, of the conflict between the gods of light (Wotan) and the gods of darkness (Alberich) bequeaths to humanity the task of establishing a universal peace.

VÖLKER   Let's now turn to another name, from another tradition, though one that also takes up the Marxist legacy, in order to transform it into a philosophical critique: Adorno. The absence of any intensive discussion between "poststructuralist" French thinking and the philosophy of critical theory has long been a source of puzzlement. And this absence seems to persist today. In the context of an ever more quickly and aggressively developing capitalism, however, the questions posed by Adorno seem to be making a return, together with the important question of the possibility of a critique of this capitalist reality in all its complexity. This raises the question of what we are to do with the critical theory of society and the negative dialectic. Now this is, of course, an enormous question, but would you agree that this problematic intersection of negativity, critique, and the relation between philosophy and society is an urgent question—one that needs to be reopened following the decline of communism as we have known it?

BADIOU For my part, I'd say that, contrary to Adorno, it's actually necessary to give a critique of the negative dialectic in order to revive the communist hypothesis. The dominant idea under Stalin was that to solve a problem it was necessary to discover—and, if necessary, create—the enemies and saboteurs preventing us from solving it. In other words, the essential element of the task was entrusted to the most violent form of negation. What we urgently need to do now is invent new forms of affirmative dialectic. In other words, affirmation was formerly confined to the imaginary register, to the invention of vague visions of a wondrous future. And the register of the real was bound up with an obsession with the enemy and the constant necessity of its destruction. What we have to do now is affirm affirmation as the very heart of the dialectic, as its real presupposition, which alone can give rise to a measured, controlled, and creative form of negation.

NANCY For my part, I'd say that Adorno has remained relatively little known in France, for two reasons. First, his thinking was obscured by the abundance of French philosophy that emerged from the beginning of the 1960s, in a country where German isn't well known and where translations take some time to appear, especially where we are talking about a style as difficult as Adorno's. Indeed, the difficulty of his style has been noted and discussed in Germany itself, and this difficulty can only increase in translation. In my view, a fundamental question remains concerning what is certainly not "jargon," but rather a certain hermeticism that cannot simply be ignored, unlike Heidegger's hermeticisms or what we might call Derrida's, or indeed Deleuze's, unreadabilities. In any case, there is certainly a general question concerning contemporary philosophical language. Badiou, for his part, represents a particular case, since in him the hermetic dimension is embedded within mathematics and psychoanalysis. At first sight, that disburdens the philosophical, but it doesn't prevent it from invoking mathematico-psychoanalytic resources.

But please forgive the digression. There is, of course, also a deeper reason—one that brings us back to the beginning of our discussion. After 1933, Germany lost its philosophers: either they emigrated or they almost all fell silent if they didn't follow the regime. One alone became the "archi-fascist," but he had raised the decisive "question of being." In exile in America, critical theory maintained a certain critical Marxist continuity. In France, this mode of thinking didn't enjoy the same force. Following Daniel Bensaïd, one could speak here of a long-term divorce between the radicalism of a social movement marked by workerism (whose heritage stretches from revolutionary trade unionism to the Communist Party of the 1930s) and those university intellectuals steeped in the positivist tradition who remained obstinately resistant to German philosophy and dialectic. The Republic on the one hand and various marginal Marxisms (such as those propounded by Bataille and Lefebvre) on the other tended rather to favor the emergence of a complex ensemble that situated its critique on another plane, largely dependent on Heideggerian deconstruction. As it happens, that's another example of the way in which philosophers don't simply spring up like mushrooms! Here it would also be necessary to retrace Althusser's whole development and to reconstruct the intellectual climate of the 1960s from Althusser to Badiou, by way of a great many others.

Where Adorno himself is concerned, however, there is also a paradox. For in the very same '60s in which he wrote his *Negative Dialectics*, he was far less distant than we tend to think from Heidegger, on the one hand, and certain supposedly "French" (and partly "Heideggerian") tendencies, on the other. In particular, I think that what separated Germany and France then was a certain relation to science and epistemology. In France, Bachelard, Cavaillès, Canguilhem—to name just a few of the leading lights—represented a non-metaphysical emancipation that lacked a significant counterpart in Germany. Around the beginning of the 1960s, we were all animated by a certain idea of science, whereas in Germany science was regarded more suspiciously on account of its ideological malleability. Derrida invented a "grammatology" in a way that was both playful and serious. The word "epistemology" was on everyone's lips (even if it was used rather indiscriminately). Foucault spoke of the "episteme" (which was also a response to the rupturing of history). In this context, the Marxists found themselves in a very difficult position, which, incidentally, explains Althusser's "epistemological break."

But Adorno was never far away. Lyotard read him closely, for example, and Miguel Abensour is far from having ignored him. Alex Garcia Düttmann (who is as French as he is German and Catalan) was very close to Derrida and has continually referred to Adorno. Adorno's *Aesthetic Theory* certainly overshadowed his *Negative Dialectics*, but the two are linked. Beyond his aesthetics, Adorno particularly attracted the attention of those concerned with the idea of a *praxis* freed from the traditional theory/practice schemas, that is, those who might concur with a statement such as "nothing can even be experienced as living if it does not also contain a promise of something transcending life," as Adorno puts it in his eighteenth lecture on metaphysics.* Now I know that the words "life" and "transcending" will immediately cause certain "poststructuralists" or "postmodernists" (to use these rather simplistic labels) to recoil. What separates France and Germany between the 1960s and the 1980s is a marked difference in the confidence placed in words. Although both sides had an uneasy and sometimes tortured sense

*Theodor W. Adorno, *Metaphysics: Concept and Problems*, ed. Rolf Tiedemann, trans. Edmund Jephcott (Cambridge: Polity, 2000), 145.

of the exigency of words—their weight, their risks, and their insufficiencies—the French developed a pronounced taste for lexical suspicion or for invention (in the manner of Deleuze or Derrida, for instance) and for the creation of styles of philosophical expression. In part, that's a Heideggerian legacy. As I suggested, Adorno also developed a certain style, yet it was more syntactical than lexical.

Be that as it may, let me conclude with the following word: to transcend. If there is anything that ceaselessly questions Franco-German or Germano-French thinking, it's this. Alain won't agree with me on this, but I would say that his immanence transcends itself quite manifestly. I admit, however, that it would be much better to do without this conceptual pair, though not without leaping outside, into the other, the elsewhere, and the infinite.

VÖLKER To close, let us turn to a rather delicate name: Heidegger. For you, Alain, Heidegger was a Nazi, but nonetheless one of the most important philosophers of the twentieth century. Perhaps you would agree with that view, Jean-Luc? Yet can Heidegger's Nazism be kept out of his philosophy? What are we to do with Heidegger? And a further, related question: Is it possible to conceive a fascist philosophy? Can thinking not only be corrupted by but also be fundamentally oriented around the idea of the primacy of a people or a race, even in its conception of being and its appearance? Finally, does the name Heidegger mark a certain displacement in Franco-German philosophical relations—a displacement that doesn't cease to displace itself?

BADIOU   Regarding Heidegger, I'd just like to say three things. First, Heidegger is the one who brought the question of being back into the space of contemporary philosophy. It was a question that, especially under the combined effect of the Kantian critique and the positivism dominant in the nineteenth century, had been forgotten, lost. Yes, that's one of the damaging consequences of Kant that you don't want to acknowledge: it was Kant who, with the appearance of the greatest rigor, said: let's not trouble ourselves with the theoretical question of being *qua* being, since theoretical thought can neither clearly formulate this problem nor resolve it. OK, let's not reopen the question of Kant. In any case, the great Heidegger brought back the question of being. He brought it back, of course, as both a complex and circumscribed question, but also as a question enclosed within a German heritage. Which means that he brought it back as an essentially historical question, and not simply, or indeed at all, as an epistemological or philosophico-conceptual question. For Heidegger, the question of being ultimately becomes something like the secret organization of human historicity. Now I have to admit that the "Heideggerian jargon" denounced by Adorno had an extremely important influence on me. I think that it was right, necessary, and imperative to bring the question of being *qua* being back to the surface of philosophical thinking. Even if my approach here is quite different from yours (put very crudely, mathematics *contra* history), I would say that Heidegger's restoration of the question of being to the surface of elementary philosophical concerns was and remains an essential gesture.

The second point is that, in bringing back the question of being, Heidegger introduced a form of torsion into the phenomenological heritage. In a certain sense, he exceeded the pure Husserlian figure, which remained in some respects dependent on psychology, as Sartre's use of it made clear. Husserl tied hermeneutical questioning to the constitutive configuration of the subject—not at the level of the transcendental categories, as in Kant, but rather at that of intentionality and temporization. Heidegger then leaves behind the epistemological and psychological question of consciousness in favor of a question that he formulates as the question of *Dasein*, which is both larger and more incisive, precisely because it is connected to the question of being.

The third point is that all of this powerful speculative material was exposed by Heidegger to an identitarian catastrophe. I would agree with you in speaking here, in relation to his German nationalism and crude anti-Semitism, of the banality of Heidegger. He was really a conventional German anti-Semite. But for me his major theoretical gesture—his contemporary reaffirmation of the question of being—is not effaced by the sociopolitical personage of the minor, provincial, anti-Semitic professor who believed for some years that Hitler was preparing for Germany, and so for Professor Heidegger himself, a destiny that could only be compared to that of Parmenides's Greece.

NANCY Things are extremely complicated here, but perhaps first of all I would say that it's not enough just to say: "Heidegger, a great moment of thinking, the question of being, but otherwise ... and that shows a fault or weakness ..." No! That's not enough. On the one hand, yes, that's how it is. And that could be illustrated by a posthumous fragment of Bataille's that I like very much, where he says, "Ultimately, Heidegger and I are talking about the same thing, but the difference is that he is a professor." Bataille puts it less aggressively than you, but it's still very aggressive on his part. But when Bataille says, "Heidegger and I are talking about the same thing," what does he ultimately mean? I think we can capture that with a word that looms large in Bataille and in your own work, and that many of us in fact share today: the *impossible*. I mean the impossible not in the sense of that which is not possible, but rather that which falls outside the calculation of possibilities— that which exceeds the possible. So I would say that what Bataille intuits here is very interesting, namely that Heidegger is perhaps the first to really introduce the impossible into philosophy. He doesn't call it that, even though at times he's not far from doing so, such as when he says that "to will the possible is not to will."

At the same time, there is a certain solidarity between what isn't simply the Nazi event, but also the overwhelming of Europe, and the overwhelming within Europe of the very relation to what is known as "politics." In essence, fascism amounts to the dismissal of politics, or rather to its absorption through the declaration that "everything is political." Heidegger was perfectly well aware of that, and he criticized the slogan "everything is political." He didn't simply commit a "great blunder," as he himself said, and one that would be the product of a rather narrow mind.

There is something else at work here. Heidegger reso-
nated with his time, his whole time. That's why he raised
the question of being. And we have to add that he was a
Nazi—yes, we all know the photo with the insignia, he was
in the party—only, very quickly, he became a hyper-Nazi.
Philippe Lacoue-Labarthe called him an archi-fascist, and
a hyper-Nazi, which would be even worse. And yet at the
same time, there's also something else. I'll leave to one
side the question of anti-Semitism, which is in fact the
question of banality—there, agreed, things really plummet.
But when we read the same *Black Notebooks* that contain
these anti-Semitic statements, when we read the *Beiträge*,
we find—I don't know quite what to call that—an extraordinary form of philosophical hyperbole. And today, when we
are beginning to gain a little distance from Heidegger, we
can only say that he already condemned what we are now
confronted with. Aside from the question of technology,
perhaps, he posed questions that haven't been discussed
since—questions that neither you nor I have discussed,
because it's extremely difficult to do so, but which I think
we philosophers should really try to discuss today. Heidegger clearly saw something, and though his thinking on
technology is always reduced to the exploitation of nature
as a stock, it's not that simple, since he himself says that
technology is also the last sending of being.

I am not at all saying that we should forget the
anti-Semitism—absolutely not. But we also mustn't forget
that Heidegger wanted this text to be published. And we
mustn't forget, too, that in the *Black Notebooks* there are

many things that are sometimes unbelievably hysterical; we sense that Heidegger is distraught, since he really does have the feeling that the world is falling apart—and he wasn't the only one at the time.

Second, then: being. Yes, absolutely. Except that what seems to me most important in Heidegger's formulation of the question of being is that he demands—though he writes it infrequently, because it's not very workable—that being not be treated as a noun, but only as a verb, and that this verb be understood as a transitive verb. And I have to say that that's something I can't shake off so easily. How are we to articulate, "is, it is that is, that is"—"that is not but that allows to exist"? There is a section in *Was ist das—die Philosophie?* where he says that we could perhaps attempt something similar with *Lesen* in the sense of gathering and of course reading. *Being = gathering, reading.* In the Anaximander Fragment, and again in the most recent volume of the *Black Notebooks*, he also says that being *braucht* beings. *Brauchen* means both to use and to need. And in the *Anaximander Fragment* he comments on a form of *Brauchen* that he himself takes as a translation of the Greek word *chreôn*, and he also uses *frui, fruor*, which he sees as equivalent to *Brauchen* in Augustine. And that yields: "being enjoys beings." So we are back to *jouissance* again. To enjoy something—is that strictly transitive? Let's say it is, let's take it as a transitive form: "Being enjoys beings." I'm not sure what to say about that. Yet there is something here— and I know I'm moving farther and farther away from you— that seems to me highly inspiring. And this inspiration, which for me is extremely strong and right [*juste*], is also that which perhaps runs up against Heidegger's political and more-than-political errancy in his attempt to grasp this: that the totality of beings, that all that there is (and that is still what interests us other philosophers) is itself trans-fixed, if you will, not by a subject, nor by a substantivized being, but transfixed, enjoyed. And here there is something that at least contains a philosophical appeal I can't ignore, though of course I don't understand it. I don't even know why Heidegger himself continually falls back into using the noun *being*, in the form of *Seyn* with a "y." Sometimes the cross he uses to strike it out returns in the fourth volume of the *Black Notebooks*. But in Heidegger there are certain curious internal contradictions between being-is-not, being-under-erasure, *being* with a "y" (which is intended to give voice to something at the heart of every concept, every substantivization of being, but which nonetheless functions as the subject of a proposition), and *being* taken strictly as a transitive verb.

BADIOU The extraordinary difficulty of ontology is that one has to be coolly convinced that an effective thinking of being requires us to acknowledge that being is wholly indif-ferent to what happens to us. When being was thought in terms of the gods, the latter were fundamentally concerned with what happens to us. Look at the Christian God! He goes so far as to die on the cross to save us. Being in Heideg-ger's sense also lies at the heart of the destiny of human-ity, which forms one of its epochs. It's clear, then, that the positing of being as absolutely indifferent to what happens to the featherless biped—being as the multiple form of all that exists and occurs, without privileging anything whatsoever—is a rupture that remains to come. Being in this sense has nothing to do with destiny and is in no way tied to the singularity of thinking humanity; on the contrary, it is the underlying register of our being, in its indifference to the destiny of humanity. To accept this indifference, we have to think and affirm that there is no history of being. What there is, is being's own unfolding as the indifferent multiplicity of multiplicities. The limitation of Heidegger's return to the question of being is his implicit perpetuation of a phenomenological vision, that is, one that consists in claiming that being has a *sense*. Strictly speaking, however, being *qua* being has no sense. It has a truth that we can approximate through mathematics, but no sense. In Heidegger's crucial gesture I see an adherence to a certain teleology that allows us to confront the destiny of being in the figures of forgetting, the forgetting of forgetting, primordial reversal, and so on. But in my view that's all a neo-religious fable, since the truth is that being has no particular concern for our own destiny as human animals on a medium-sized planet, orbiting an average-sized star, in a very ordinary galaxy. And the thought of being *qua* being is—in the form of modern set theory, for example—the epitome of a thinking that is disconnected from what happens to us. What matters here is to examine, in a way that is ultimately both rational and disinterested, the possible forms of any multiplicity whatsoever. And yet, it was only in a space opened by the Heideggerian question that I was able to arrive at this mathematical vision of the indifference of being.

NANCY Yes, but I find that the more you speak, the closer you come to Heidegger himself. If Heidegger says that being enjoys beings, is that not precisely to say something about the indifference you're speaking of ...

BADIOU I don't really see ...

NANCY But yes—because it means that, since being isn't a subject and doesn't produce, it is *jouissance*—let's keep this word for a moment—it is the *jouissance* of the multiplicity in its ...

BADIOU But what does *jouissance* have to do with anything? A differential equation doesn't really enjoy anything.

NANCY Yes, but so much the worse for it.

BADIOU Absolutely, so much the worse for it, and for us, and especially for your *jouissance*.

NANCY No, not at all, since we can enjoy a differential equation.

BADIOU Ah, but be careful! *We* can enjoy a differential equation, but a differential equation itself doesn't enjoy anything. We can sometimes enjoy the indifference of being, too—that's always possible. We have invented all sorts of perversions.

NANCY If you like, *jouissance* is essentially a hyperbolic word, a dangerous one that stands in for sense. For

Heidegger, the question of being is the question of the sense of being.

BADIOU   For Heidegger, yes, but it's there that he goes astray. The question of being, on the contrary, amounts to finally working up the courage to rationally confront what has no sense. Previously, in the Heideggerian tradition, what had no sense was practically intolerable. It was the absurd, it was the terrible existential operation of confronting non-sense, it was Sartre's nausea. That's what the question of being was as a question of sense. But the truth is that being has no sense, that's all. It is what it is, insofar as we can rationally and disinterestedly elaborate a mathematics of any multiplicity whatsoever. There is neither *jouissance*, nor sense, nor anything else of the sort. There are cleverly coded forms of writing, and that's all there is.

NANCY   But in saying that you forget Derrida, who took up the question of being as a question of the difference between being and beings, naming it "*différance*" with an "a"—the *différance* of being or being differing from itself. Now people wrote a lot about this word, disparaging and often getting worked up about it, wanting to understand it as the continual deferral of what was about to take place, as though Derrida were saying "Free beer tomorrow," "Free thinking tomorrow," or "Free *jouissance* tomorrow." But I think that with this *différance* with an "a" (it's of course also something written) Derrida precisely wanted to draw something out of Adorno's statement, "No being without beings." Now, of course, there is no being without beings, but that's also a statement that remains very faithful to Heidegger, while passing through time and multiplicity. What takes place? Things take place. Multiplicity takes place in its contingency. Events take place—you would be the first to insist on that. In Derrida's *différance*, one might say that Heidegger's being is taken up again otherwise, or reconceived, and its difference from beings is at once annulled, displaced, and transported. And you yourself grant that some importance—when you say you will write "*inexistance*" with an "a," you grant to Derrida that a gerund in place of a noun changes something. And there is indeed something very important there. A gerund is something that is in the process of taking place. This "in-the-process-of" is something that English possesses in a remarkable manner—to such an extent that in English gerunds themselves often become nouns. Now the indifference you speak of, including the indifference of the differential equation, this indifference is the real; it is really in the process of taking place. This real that Lacan calls impossible, as you have noted from time to time, is impossible in the sense that it falls outside the calculation of the possible. For me, that amounts to thinking, via the Derridean operation and *différance*, not an indifference that as you describe it resembles the indifference of the Epicurean gods, but what I call *sense*. Epicurus says, "The gods are over there and they don't care what happens to us." But no, it's not that being doesn't care what happens to us; since it's not someone, it neither cares nor doesn't care. So this indifference in the sense of sense—because it's perhaps simply a verbal dispute here, since you understand "sense" as "sense that has a final signification"—is also found there where something takes place. I don't have another word for it; what I understand by "sense" is the simple fact that something takes place, that it refers from one point to another. And that's something else that I take from Heidegger. When Heidegger says that the world is a totality of *Bedeutsamkeit* (which Martineau translates as *significabilité*), then this is an aptitude, a capacity to *bedeuten*, but it's not a given *Bedeutung*. That the world is a totality of *Bedeutsamkeit* means simply that it is a totality that is not to be understood in a totalitarian sense, but rather as the entirety of all that takes place and can take place, and that does not cease to refer to itself as the impossible that falls outside any calculation of possibility. I call that a sense, but I don't insist on the word. I do think, though, that it makes a difference [*écart*] whether we speak of sense or indifference.

BADIOU   For me, it's a considerable difference. Between indifference and sense, I see a genuine abyss. But I wonder whether we shouldn't call a halt at the edge of this abyss, as I sense that exhaustion is gaining the upper hand!

VÖLKER   One very last question. To pursue this difference between being and sense or sense and indifference: Is there a contemporary configuration of this difference, or does the question of the contemporary not touch on it? What role does the figure of the contemporary play in a philosophy based on the question of being? And to return again to a Heideggerian problematic, without reopening the question of Heidegger: is it possible to question or consider whether there is a task for contemporary philosophy that is specifically tied to the Franco-German philosophical tradition?

BADIOU What I can say is that the work of thinking, with respect to the difference between being, sense, and indifference, or between conceptual rationality and historical intuition, in relation to the human comprehension of being *qua* being, is characteristic of a certain distanced complicity or fraternal contradiction between German and French thought. And we bear witness to that: after the French infatuation with German thought (exemplified by Sartre and Derrida) and the distance separating French structuralism and German hermeneutics, what we can now expect to emerge is a new form of this work of thinking, one that I think will address the following problem: how are we to reconstruct an affirmative dialectic on the basis of an ontology that accepts the indifference of being? Yes, I think that's a problem we have in common.

NANCY Let me respond very resolutely: yes. Because I think that the difference between being and sense or between indifference and sense first of all amounts to a difference between being and being, or a difference within being. This difference, which I find in Heidegger's suggestion of playing the (transitive) verb against the noun, in the "a" of Derrida's *différance*, in Adorno's "no being without beings," and in the "anything whatsoever" of multiplicity in Badiou—this difference is itself the result of the contemporary. The contemporary is this time that has become isomorphic and isochronic with itself, a time that only orients itself privatively in relation to its past and future, without thereby possessing a tangible eternity, a time suspended along a narrow ridge.

This contemporary is also the time of the global closure of a (technological, economic, cultural) logic of civilization, which is beginning to doubt itself, that is, to doubt what "being" has implied ever since Plato's *ousia* (though we shouldn't forget that Plato also speaks of an *epekeina tès ousias*). And it seems quite plausible that this time is a response to Plato's in the form of its suspension and mutation. Twenty-six centuries, that's enough for a civilization. From Marx and Nietzsche to Heidegger, there have been no lack of signs of its collapse: Lenin, Freud, Einstein, Husserl ... and Heidegger represents a turning point here, since it was in him that this malaise crystallized around "being." Where everyone else saw progress and an advance (even if critically), he brought together all of the characteristics and the whole problem of the Occident under the heading of ontology. One might say that it is with Heidegger that the notion of the contemporary as the time suspended in itself emerges as the driving force and motive of philosophy—to such an extent that it even prompts talk of the end of philosophy. Since Heidegger's time, we have remained in a state of suspension. Not without movement, to be sure, but this movement has been difficult and hesitant, as is to be expected in a time when all assurances have been shaken or become suspect, to say the least.

Even Heidegger's anti-Semitism—his lamentable recourse to a banal element of his time—bears witness to something, since anti-Semitism is a foundational element of our Romano-Christian culture, one that involves certain basic motives oriented around a form of division and self-rejection of an "Occidental" identity. And Heidegger represents the high point of such self-criticism or self-hatred, which, incidentally, had been rather alien to philosophy before Marx and Nietzsche. It's a remarkable trait that divides Heidegger against himself at the root.

Perhaps one might say that a complex, chiasmatic division between being and sense indeed marks the contemporaneity of a Franco-German combinatorics in which philosophy unfolds—or at least a philosophy that does not renounce being or sense, that does not simply dismiss ontology in favor of a consideration of "forms of language" or "forms of life." I'm not rejecting Wittgenstein here; I only think there is something else at stake in philosophy, something rooted in a "real irreducible to the fiction of something hidden," as Alain said in our discussion.

Now I adhere to the exigency of this "real-real," as it were—which in fact is not simply an exigency but ultimately philosophical passion itself (in a sense recalled by the Husserlian injunction to return "to the things themselves"). The real as being and/or sense, as the chiasm of the two. And this is attested to by the contemporary dominance—in contexts that tend to lie outside of this Franco-German combinatorics—of a vogue for the "real" that goes by such names as "new realism," "speculative realism," or "object-oriented philosophy." Now this movement assumes that philosophy has remained enclosed within subjectivity, and that everything else has been considered in relation or relative to it. But that's an extremely naïve supposition. Thinking has never been concerned with a "subject" in a unilateral relation to "objects"—even in Descartes and even in Kant. Everything has always commenced and recommenced with being-in-the-world, with being thrown into a world that is neither given nor guaranteed, yet absolutely existent.

Afterword

Jan Völker

In thanks to Alain Badiou and Jean-Luc Nancy and to all involved in their discussion in Berlin on January 30, 2016, I should like here to add a few closing remarks—three remarks, to be precise, all of which bear on the following question: what does it mean to conduct a philosophical dialogue on German philosophy from a French perspective? I shall approach this question by way of three paradoxes.

Let us begin with the question of philosophical dialogue. A dialogue between philosophers is no simple matter. Indeed, Gilles Deleuze and Félix Guattari even famously claimed "every philosopher runs away when he or she hears someone say 'Let's discuss this.'" Deleuze the philosopher and Guattari the psychoanalyst were convinced that philosophy is badly served by discussions, since these "are fine for roundtable talks, but philosophy throws its dice on another table. The best one can say about discussions is that they take things no farther, since the participants never talk about the same thing."*

Hardly a good basis for a public dialogue between philosophers. In the above citation, however, a discussion

*Gilles Deleuze and Félix Guattari, *What Is Philosophy?*, trans. Graham Burchill and Hugh Tomlinson (New York: Columbia University Press, 1994), 28.

is understood in the very specific sense of an exchange of individual opinions whose ultimate aim is to reach a common conclusion on a given question. For Deleuze and Guattari, by contrast, the task of philosophy is rather to create concepts and to elaborate complex conceptual constructions around problems. Such conceptual work eludes discussion insofar as the latter's ever-increasing clarity reduces the space for debatable ambiguities and eventualities, and for weighing up, making concessions, and negotiating. In a word, then, the task of philosophy is precisely to create that which escapes discussion.

This raises the question of whether a dialogue between philosophers can involve anything more than the interlocutors taking turns to pronounce self-contained theses that occasionally happen to concur with one another. Beckett would be the covert master of such dialogues, such as those between Vladimir and Estragon, which oscillate between surprising and absurd agreements and ostentatious refusals to communicate, without any guarantee of a common ground.

Yet just as we do not have to interpret *Waiting for Godot* as a proof of the impossibility of dialogue, and can rather understand its dialogues as unfolding in their own obstinate way, we perhaps do not have to share Deleuze and Guattari's pessimism. It is true, of course, that philosophy is not known for its wealth of dialogues. Its history is littered with prominent refusals to engage in discussion. We might think here of an ironic Socrates, who does not shy away from exposing his interlocutor's conceptual confusion while still calling on him to keep the apparent dialogue going with so many variations on "Yes, indeed, Socrates." Yet no discussion takes place between them—neither as an exchange of opinions nor in any other form. We might also think of Derrida's or Adorno's texts. Certain attempts to understand them, that is, to treat them as addresses to the reader, only result in them retreating further inside themselves and carrying on a game of their own. At a crucial moment, they withdraw from communicative exchange. Finally, we might think of Hegel, who at the opening of the *Phenomenology of Spirit* contrasts the individual expression of opinion with universal truth. Language outstrips individual opinion because it necessarily expresses a true universality; we therefore cannot even say what we individually mean. Philosophy has no interest in opinion, and even beyond the level of opinion, it does not need dialogue in the strict sense, since there is nothing opposed to the universal.

The refusal of reciprocal discussion, the refusal to enter into relation through communicative exchange, and the refusal to recognize anything opposed to oneself: these are three strategies through which philosophy undermines the very basis of dialogue. We can surely conclude, then, that the discussion of opinions about various forms of the universal is a veritable absurdity for philosophy, a motley monster of arbitrariness from which every philosopher shrinks in fear. In the good-natured, liberal exchange of ideas, in the friendly, congenial adoption of the other's arguments and the warm openness of one's own, and ultimately in the shared, mutually elaborated conception of "the essence of the matter," philosophy fears losing its own "essence [*Sache*]," namely, its capacity to draw distinctions. The discussion of opinions paves the way for consensus, and consensus building was never one of philosophy's strengths. Philosophy therefore admits no results, resolutions, or decrees, and no common, considered evaluation of things; always somewhat aloof and vain, it makes few friends.

Yet if on the one hand philosophy evades and even fears dialogue, on the other it is always an address to everyone and continually seeks to realize itself as such. It is an eminently rational affair, a discourse of reason and argument conducted in the conviction that it is possible to speak with anyone whatsoever. It therefore avoids recourse or reference to esoteric, invisible sources and reasons via verifiable proofs and logical chains. As a rational discourse, philosophy aims to secure the other's assent; it welcomes the well-founded argument and seeks progress in thinking. In its very rationality, then, it turns toward the public sphere, and it is in this public domain that it exhibits its rationality. It is thus a rational praxis. Socrates did not shrink from a single discursive debate; his entire philosophy consists in dialogues. Many of Derrida's books were initially given as talks. Adorno willingly made many radio appearances, and even Hegel was essentially a lecturing philosopher. Philosophy cannot do without public speaking; it is impelled toward and needs the public sphere. In its very essence, it is a public activity, and even the book is a mode of writing that is oriented toward the public domain—one that reflects on praxis by drawing it back inside itself. From this perspective, then, there is no private philosophy—no philosophy that is not public from the outset, that has not already left the private sphere and begun to seek out a praxis as soon as it begins to think.

But what exactly does it mean to call the public domain a condition of philosophical thinking? Does philosophy need a large audience, a packed marketplace? The problem here can be illustrated by a striking scene from Plato's *Protagoras*, in which the young Hippocrates asks Socrates to put in a good word for him with the sophist Protagoras, in the hope of being taken on as his student. They resolve to visit the sophist in order first to clarify what Hippocrates would be taught. When they find Protagoras, he insists that their conversation about the content of his teaching should take place in public, since as a sophist he aims to educate others. Since the sophist's speech aims to educate, and thus requires the other as an interlocutor, one might then say that the sophists are public speakers *par excellence*. In Plato's dialogues, however, they are continually shown up as not knowing precisely what they claim to know. Hippias, another sophist, wears himself out with his various attempts to define beauty, all of which rest on particular examples and fail to accede to the level of the universal. The sophists can neither give a substantial justification for their beliefs nor unite these various views on the beautiful, virtue, or thinking into any form of essence, since they ultimately all remain at the level of the individual example. And since this generates a state of inconclusiveness in which examples are multiplied and knowledge has to be continually refined, the sophists are in fact caught up in what might be called the privacy of particular beliefs.

It is then ultimately the sophist who, though speaking before a large audience, thinks privately rather than publicly. Forced into a corner by Socrates, Hippias has to ask for a few minutes to reflect; he needs to step back from the dialogue to reconsider his own beliefs. Plato thus exposes the sophist as someone who teaches publicly but thinks privately, whereas the philosopher thinks publicly but does not need a large audience to do so: he thinks via debate. Indeed, he thinks debate and distinction as such, which is why, as Socrates repeatedly notes, he has no particular content of his own that he could teach. The philosopher focuses on knowledge in order to question it, and perhaps in doing so he changes it, but he neither possesses nor presents his own knowledge. To borrow a phrase of Kant's, the philosopher makes public use of his reason. Yet to think publicly in this way is always already to reflect on public matters, since these are objects of debate with any given other. In this fundamental sense, philosophy is always a form of dialogue and debate.

For the philosopher, then, dialogue is the most natural thing in the world, and dialogue is public from the outset. Yet this yields a rather complex image of philosophy, since it now proves to be both vain and aloof *and* a public act of thinking. Philosophy is a rational, public debate with anyone and everyone about public matters, yet one that that not only escapes any individualizing discussion of the matter at hand but also its practical summation in an easily communicable form of knowledge. We might then say that philosophy disturbs public communication through a public act, while having the temerity to do so in a wholly transparent manner. In Plato, this form of dialogue—this contradictory, public act of thinking—is called *dialectic*.

It is not hard to see that in today's universal public sphere, where philosophy represents a singular voice of exception, this attitude is not particularly well regarded. Philosophy occupies a difficult position insofar as it undermines knowledge and confronts it with an idea that cannot directly serve its pursuit. It generates useless questions, it generates problems, and it subdivides what is seemingly one and the same time. On top of everything, it does so in a rational, structured manner, unfolding the endless complications of things, relieving them of their apparent simplicity and habitual usage, and even transforming our knowledge of them. In a word: it makes distinctions.

We can then summarize the first paradox of philosophical dialogue as follows: philosophy seeks a rational dialogue that rejects practical results and communication through the multiplication of distinctions, to such an extent that its unwieldiness carries over into the very forms of its discourse. Insofar as it is a rational discourse, it is then intelligible, and insofar as it eludes communication through the continual multiplication of distinctions, it is unintelligible. There is no philosophy without debate; the philosopher is always in debate with the thoughts and things confronting her. There can then also be a dialogue *between* philosophers just because they do not speak about the same thing. Such genuine dialogue, however, is marked more by contradictions and unrelated juxtapositions than by figures of mutual understanding. And it is by following this roundabout path that philosophical dialogue ultimately leads to an ambivalent form of agreement—one that pertains to the shared* essence of philosophy: its will to distinction.

Yet if philosophy only speaks insofar as it distinguishes, then this contradictory dimension of philosophical dialogue already hints at a further contradiction. Philosophy not only engages in a distinctive form of debate; at the formal level, it also continually oscillates between the spoken and the written word. It comes from writing, it is on its way to writing, and it needs writing in order to overcome the transience of the spoken word by inscribing itself in reality. It therefore needs the book. The dialogue first comes back to itself as a book, perhaps because the reader may regret not having been there to witness it in person, so that a certain interval emerges. And it is within this very interval—in which speech is already on its way to writing, to losing itself in writing—that philosophy charts its course.

Whether Socrates would have been a philosopher without Plato is no simple question. Let us nonetheless

---

*[The German here is *geteilt*, which, like the French *partagé*, can mean both shared and divided. Though I have generally chosen to translate it as "shared" (except where indicated otherwise), in many instances it can also be read as "divided."—Trans.]

suggest that, in a strict sense, he would not. For the book is another form, and one that essentially belongs to philosophy. A philosophy requires written inscriptions to sustain the very presence that it constructs through dialogue. This philosophical presence is weak, and it risks vanishing with the dialogue in the mere course of time. The book sustains this philosophical presence, and in the movement between speech and writing philosophy constructs a presence that enters into debate with the present in which it finds itself. The philosophical inscriptions set down in books are not timeless propositions, but rather the result of their time, that is, the result of dialogues on public questions. The book is thus a necessary support for the weak voice, yet is itself no end point, since it only constitutes a further form of public address. And that is precisely the problem of the book: though it retains that which exceeds the contingency of individual opinions and the arbitrariness of passing time, it also threatens to turn philosophy into a form of knowledge that apparently lies outside time. Philosophy would then be something that could be taught and would no longer depend on debate. Yet philosophy lives on debate, while at the same time evading it, just as it produces books that subsequently require further debate. The book continues a complex, circuitous dialogue that circumvents mere opinion and progresses by way of contradictions and discontinuities; it is itself an element of dialogue. Herein lies the second paradox of philosophical dialogue: it is always already bound for the book, since it always already transcends the given moment; and yet the book itself is not its terminus, but just another turning point in the overall discussion.

Somewhere between an elitist intractability that conceives itself as a universal address and a form of speech that is always already bound for the book (without conceiving it as its terminus), the figure of the philosophical dialogue thus begins to emerge. This dialogue constructs its own space through a debate that avoids and recoils from the exchange of opinions and knowledge and continually oscillates between the book and the spoken word. It is a zigzag line that not only circumscribes its own space but also its very own temporality.

The essence of philosophy lies in this very shared space and temporality. This sharing traditionally finds expression in concepts—in the concept of the Idea, for example, which is shared by both Plato and Hegel. It also finds expression in the sharing of problems—such as the problem of language shared by Derrida and Adorno. Concepts and problems, moreover, continually refer to one another: if concepts are instruments for making distinctions, problems refer to the space of concepts. The dialogue is divided up into the intractability of the concept and the public character of the problem, just as the written text develops the concept that it inscribes as speech within a public problem. Finally, the shared essence of philosophy, in the space and present between the concept and the problem, also finds expression in a certain constellation, since it amounts to a debate with others. Plato, for example, shares the public sphere as a contested space with the sophists. Within such constellations, shared concepts and problems open up specific philosophical periods.

It is in these periods that the third paradox of philosophy emerges: the spatiotemporal unfolding of its thinking body. This is a complex process that generates a host of problematic names. What, indeed, is meant by "idealism," or "structuralism"? Or, even more problematically, by "German philosophy" or "French philosophy"? Such names surely at first only sow confusion. National philosophers? Have we not come a little further than that?

If we approach philosophy along the branching lines of concepts, problems, and constellations and the intersecting fissures marked in speech and books, then we would increasingly have to ask what these names refer to. Do they express the commonality of an identity? Or does "German philosophy," like "French philosophy," not first of all refer to a contradictory constellation? Alain Badiou opens the foregoing discussion by dividing philosophy up into a chain of discontinuous periods, which he terms "Greek," "German," and "French." He nonetheless includes Leibniz and Spinoza in the seventeenth-century "French" period. Jean-Luc Nancy, in turn, notes the difficulties Kant experienced in writing in a language that did not allow his thinking to unfold as he wished. Kant remained ensnared in an antiquated German, while at the same time being deeply attached to it.

The content of "German" or "French" philosophy is then defined neither by linguistic nor by national borders. Let us not then seek to understand "German philosophy" and "French philosophy" too hastily as denoting identities, but rather as indicating the broad frameworks of complex debates. As a universal mode of address, philosophy cannot be contained within national borders, nor even within the limits of a national language; it nonetheless takes a variety of forms that are often externally distinguished by their language. Furthermore, figures such as "German philosophy" and "French philosophy" tend to resurface through their various reinterpretations. In the foregoing dialogue, "German philosophy" comes into view through its reinterpretation by "French philosophy." In this reinterpretation, it clearly assumes a very particular form, which differs from other manifestations of "German philosophy" in other discourses.

What, then, are "German" philosophy and "French" philosophy? Certainly not one or another of their manifestations, but rather the entirety of their consequences. There is nonetheless no definitive consensus as to what these are. Nancy, for example, notes the famous displacement that takes place between French and German philosophy in the wake of the French Revolution. German philosophy came to be marked by a certain distance, in the form of an expectation or fear of another revolution, or an attempt to foment it. And as Badiou remarks, a similar intersection gave rise to the contemporary "French" philosophical period, which was initially marked by a renewed engagement with German thinkers. Terms such as "German philosophy" and "French philosophy" describe complex constellations that, while referring to languages and nation states, above all play host to shared concepts and problems, though these take a range of forms. Perhaps this is why they can only reveal their full import in translation. Perhaps it is only then that they can appear in their true structure—not falsified as in some discussions, not in the form of the orthodoxies and dogmatisms of those who believe in unchanging knowledge, but rather in their essential import, which manifests itself in translation as a renewal of their distinguishing power. The translation of one philosophy into another thus develops what it traces back to its essential import. It renews and rejuvenates it by repeating its distinctions. It conducts a dialogue; it writes philosophy's present.

What does it mean, then, to conduct a dialogue on German philosophy from a French perspective? It means, first of all, to exhibit the presence of philosophy, to share its essence, to develop problems by debating shared concepts. It means to rejuvenate its thinking body. A dialogue, then, is always an address, a praxis—an invitation, a letter.